This Cleaning Planner belongs to

Yearly Cleaning

January

-
-
-
-
-
-
-
-
-

February

-
-
-
-
-
-
-
-
-

March

-
-
-
-
-
-
-
-
-

April

-
-
-
-
-
-
-
-

May

-
-
-
-
-
-
-
-

June

-
-
-
-
-
-
-
-

Yearly Cleaning

January

-
-
-
-
-
-
-
-

February

-
-
-
-
-
-
-
-

March

-
-
-
-
-
-
-
-

April

-
-
-
-
-
-
-
-

May

-
-
-
-
-
-
-
-

June

-
-
-
-
-
-
-
-

Yearly Cleaning

Tasks	J	F	M	A	M	J	J	A	S	O	N	D

Yearly Cleaning

Tasks	J	F	M	A	M	J	J	A	S	O	N	D

Cleaning list

Bedroom

Living room

Closets

Cleaning list

Kitchen

Outdoor

Other

Daily Cleaning

Tasks	Mon	Tue	Wed	Thu	Fri	Sat	Sun

Supplies

Daily Cleaning

Tasks	Mon	Tue	Wed	Thu	Fri	Sat	Sun

Supplies

Cleaning list

Bedroom

Living room

Closets

Cleaning list

Kitchen

Outdoor

Other

Daily Cleaning

Tasks	Mon	Tue	Wed	Thu	Fri	Sat	Sun

Supplies

Daily Cleaning

Tasks	Mon	Tue	Wed	Thu	Fri	Sat	Sun

Supplies

Cleaning list

Bedroom

Living room

Closets

Cleaning list

Kitchen

Outdoor

Other

Daily Cleaning

Tasks	Mon	Tue	Wed	Thu	Fri	Sat	Sun

Supplies

Daily Cleaning

Tasks	Mon	Tue	Wed	Thu	Fri	Sat	Sun

Supplies

Cleaning list

Bedroom

Living room

Closets

Cleaning list

Kitchen

Outdoor

Other

Daily Cleaning

Tasks	Mon	Tue	Wed	Thu	Fri	Sat	Sun

Supplies

Daily Cleaning

Tasks	Mon	Tue	Wed	Thu	Fri	Sat	Sun

Supplies

Cleaning list

Bedroom

Living room

Closets

Cleaning list

Kitchen

Outdoor

Other

Daily Cleaning

Tasks	Mon	Tue	Wed	Thu	Fri	Sat	Sun

Supplies

Daily Cleaning

Tasks	Mon	Tue	Wed	Thu	Fri	Sat	Sun

Supplies

Cleaning list

Bedroom

Living room

Closets

Cleaning list

Kitchen

Outdoor

Other

Daily Cleaning

Tasks	Mon	Tue	Wed	Thu	Fri	Sat	Sun

Supplies

Daily Cleaning

Tasks	Mon	Tue	Wed	Thu	Fri	Sat	Sun

Supplies

Cleaning list

Bedroom

Living room

Closets

Cleaning list

Kitchen

Outdoor

Other

Daily Cleaning

Tasks	Mon	Tue	Wed	Thu	Fri	Sat	Sun

Supplies

Daily Cleaning

Tasks	Mon	Tue	Wed	Thu	Fri	Sat	Sun

Supplies

Cleaning list

Bedroom

Living room

Closets

Cleaning list

Kitchen

Outdoor

Other

Daily Cleaning

Tasks	Mon	Tue	Wed	Thu	Fri	Sat	Sun

Supplies

Daily Cleaning

Tasks	Mon	Tue	Wed	Thu	Fri	Sat	Sun

Supplies

Cleaning list

Bedroom

Living room

Closets

Cleaning list

Kitchen

Outdoor

Other

Daily Cleaning

Tasks	Mon	Tue	Wed	Thu	Fri	Sat	Sun

Supplies

Daily Cleaning

Tasks	Mon	Tue	Wed	Thu	Fri	Sat	Sun

Supplies

Cleaning list

Bedroom

Living room

Closets

Cleaning list

Kitchen

Outdoor

Other

Daily Cleaning

Tasks	Mon	Tue	Wed	Thu	Fri	Sat	Sun

Supplies

Daily Cleaning

Tasks	Mon	Tue	Wed	Thu	Fri	Sat	Sun

Supplies

Cleaning list

Bedroom

Living room

Closets

Cleaning list

Kitchen

Outdoor

Other

Daily Cleaning

Tasks	Mon	Tue	Wed	Thu	Fri	Sat	Sun

Supplies

Daily Cleaning

Tasks	Mon	Tue	Wed	Thu	Fri	Sat	Sun

Supplies

Cleaning list

Bedroom

Living room

Closets

Cleaning list

Kitchen

Outdoor

Other

Daily Cleaning

Tasks	Mon	Tue	Wed	Thu	Fri	Sat	Sun

Supplies

Daily Cleaning

Tasks	Mon	Tue	Wed	Thu	Fri	Sat	Sun

Supplies

Cleaning list

Bedroom

Living room

Closets

Cleaning list

Kitchen

Outdoor

Other

Daily Cleaning

Tasks	Mon	Tue	Wed	Thu	Fri	Sat	Sun

Supplies

Daily Cleaning

Tasks	Mon	Tue	Wed	Thu	Fri	Sat	Sun

Supplies

Cleaning list

Bedroom

Living room

Closets

Cleaning list

Kitchen

Outdoor

Other

Daily Cleaning

Tasks	Mon	Tue	Wed	Thu	Fri	Sat	Sun

Supplies

Daily Cleaning

Tasks	Mon	Tue	Wed	Thu	Fri	Sat	Sun

Supplies

Cleaning list

Bedroom

Living room

Closets

Cleaning list

Kitchen

Outdoor

Other

Daily Cleaning

Tasks	Mon	Tue	Wed	Thu	Fri	Sat	Sun

Supplies

Daily Cleaning

Tasks	Mon	Tue	Wed	Thu	Fri	Sat	Sun

Supplies

Cleaning list

Bedroom

Living room

Closets

Cleaning list

Kitchen

Outdoor

Other

Daily Cleaning

Tasks	Mon	Tue	Wed	Thu	Fri	Sat	Sun

Supplies

Daily Cleaning

Tasks	Mon	Tue	Wed	Thu	Fri	Sat	Sun

Supplies

Cleaning list

Bedroom

Living room

Closets

Cleaning list

Kitchen

Outdoor

Other

Daily Cleaning

Tasks	Mon	Tue	Wed	Thu	Fri	Sat	Sun

Supplies

Daily Cleaning

Tasks	Mon	Tue	Wed	Thu	Fri	Sat	Sun

Supplies

Cleaning list

Bedroom

Living room

Closets

Cleaning list

Kitchen

Outdoor

Other

Daily Cleaning

Tasks	Mon	Tue	Wed	Thu	Fri	Sat	Sun

Supplies

Daily Cleaning

Tasks	Mon	Tue	Wed	Thu	Fri	Sat	Sun

Supplies

Cleaning list

Bedroom

Living room

Closets

Cleaning list

Kitchen

Outdoor

Other

Daily Cleaning

Tasks	Mon	Tue	Wed	Thu	Fri	Sat	Sun

Supplies

Daily Cleaning

Tasks	Mon	Tue	Wed	Thu	Fri	Sat	Sun

Supplies

Cleaning list

Bedroom

Living room

Closets

Cleaning list

Kitchen

Outdoor

Other

Daily Cleaning

Tasks	Mon	Tue	Wed	Thu	Fri	Sat	Sun

Supplies

Daily Cleaning

Tasks	Mon	Tue	Wed	Thu	Fri	Sat	Sun

Supplies

Cleaning list

Bedroom

Living room

Closets

Cleaning list

Kitchen

Outdoor

Other

Daily Cleaning

Tasks	Mon	Tue	Wed	Thu	Fri	Sat	Sun

Supplies

Daily Cleaning

Tasks	Mon	Tue	Wed	Thu	Fri	Sat	Sun

Supplies

Cleaning list

Bedroom

Living room

Closets

Cleaning list

Kitchen

Outdoor

Other

Daily Cleaning

Tasks	Mon	Tue	Wed	Thu	Fri	Sat	Sun

Supplies

Daily Cleaning

Tasks	Mon	Tue	Wed	Thu	Fri	Sat	Sun

Supplies

Cleaning list

Bedroom

Living room

Closets

Cleaning list

Kitchen

Outdoor

Other

Daily Cleaning

Tasks	Mon	Tue	Wed	Thu	Fri	Sat	Sun

Supplies

Daily Cleaning

Tasks	Mon	Tue	Wed	Thu	Fri	Sat	Sun

Supplies

Cleaning list

Bedroom

Living room

Closets

Cleaning list

Kitchen

Outdoor

Other

Daily Cleaning

Tasks	Mon	Tue	Wed	Thu	Fri	Sat	Sun

Supplies

CPSIA information can be obtained
at www.ICGtesting.com
Printed in the USA
BVHW011129080221
599628BV00012B/1102